Genre Historical Fiction

Essential Question
What influences the development of a culture?

Wrought by Fire

by Diana Noonan
illustrated by Vaughan Flanagan

Y0-BPX-402

Chapter 1
AYZIZE LOOKS BACK

Standing ankle deep in thick mud, Ayzize hacked at the riverbank above his head. He lifted yet another heavy basket of clay onto his shoulders and winced at the weight of it. Behind him, the fast-flowing waters of the Nile tumbled over shallow outcrops of rock. On the far side, women slapped their laundry against smooth boulders, and children splashed in the shallows. Ayzize longed to leave his work and wade into the cool water. How he longed to forget the hours that stretched ahead of him. Apprenticed to a potter—and only eleven years old! How had it happened to *him*? He was the son of the great cattle herder, Ammon. It seemed only yesterday that he had been as carefree and playful as those children he now watched.

Ayzize's chest tightened. He took a few staggering steps, and his eyes filled with tears as he remembered his father. It was impossible to contain his grief. Ammon was gone. Ayzize had helped his mother to bury him, and his family's life had changed forever.

Ammon had been a tall, proud man. He was the richest farmer in the village. His cattle were strong, and his cows gave good milk. Ayzize's mother was well respected by the women in the village. Ayzize and his six brothers and sisters had everything they needed. And then the sickness arrived.

One after another, his father's animals refused to eat. Their eyes grew dull and lifeless; thick scabs formed around their mouths; they staggered and fell and finally died. Soon the neighbors' animals began to suffer the same fate. The men of the village blamed Ammon. They said he was cursed. Children shouted insults at Ayzize and his brothers and sisters and treated them with derision. His mother didn't dare leave the house. As more and more cattle died, Ayzize's family was driven from the village. Ammon built a crude shelter for them in a thicket of bushes, and soon after that, he grew ill.

Ayzize knew that his family was not cursed. Ammon had told him the real reason for the sickness. It was the strangers arriving in their land. For weeks they had been crossing the horizon with long trains of heavily laden camels.

Each night they camped on the edge of the land where Ayzize's father's cattle grazed. Others in the village kept away from these men, but Ammon visited them often. He traded milk and cheese for strange foods and beautiful fabric.

As Ammon lay on the ground inside the family's shelter, growing weaker and weaker, he spoke of having seen thick scabs around the camels' mouths. They were just like the scabs on the mouths of his cattle. He shook his head, puzzled. Why did the camels seem so strong when his cattle died? Ayzize watched Ammon grow thinner. Was his father also a victim of some new sickness the strangers had brought with them?

After Ammon's death, Ayzize and his family struggled to survive. They lived off the little dried meat his mother had preserved, and when it ran out, they collected wild berries. They drank water from the springs the cattle had once used. There seemed to be no way they could survive until, one day, Ayzize's uncle arrived. Horus was Ayzize's mother's brother. He said he had found a solution to their troubles.

"There is a potter in the next village who has no sons," Horus said. "His name is Naeem, and he's looking for an apprentice. Ayzize is old enough to work. His wages could buy you food."

Ayzize could not believe the impudence of the man! Who was he to tell the son of Ammon that he must work as a virtual servant to an artisan! He swallowed hard as his uncle continued.

"You don't have a choice," Horus said. "Your children are starving! The boy *must* be sent to work."

Even before his mother spoke, Ayzize knew what he must do. The next day, for the benefit of his family, he set out alone to the next village in search of Naeem.

The sound of the children playing in the water behind him drew Ayzize from his daydreaming. He adjusted the heavy basket of clay on his shoulders. Ugly, sticky stuff—how he loathed it! Naeem spoke of the clay as if it were a thing of promise. He rubbed his fingers through each basket that Ayzize delivered and looked at the muck lovingly.

Suddenly Ayzize felt angry. How could anything of beauty and usefulness ever come from such backbreaking work and filthy, sticky dirt? If being apprenticed to a potter were his legacy, he'd rather have been buried with his father!

STOP AND CHECK

What is Ayzize thinking about when he looks back on the past? What has changed in his life?

Chapter 2
A STRONG FOUNDATION

"Harder!" shouted Naeem from where he was working beneath the eaves of his house. "Roll harder, or there'll be bubbles in that clay. They'll burst in the oven and shatter the pot."

Ayzize felt as if he had been stung by a whip. Couldn't Naeem see that he was doing his best? His back felt as if it might break in two and his knees were raw from kneeling on the stony ground. Over the weeks, he'd worked all the hours of the day. He'd carried clay from the river. He'd mixed it with straw and spread it in the sun to dry. Now he was kneading it into long coils for Naeem to shape into pots.

Naeem left his work and came to stand beside Ayzize. "Have you ever seen a shattered pot?" he asked more gently. "It's an ugly thing. Come! I'll show you what I mean."

Ayzize followed Naeem out of the compound to a field at the edge of the village. They saw a pile of gray ash and broken pots. How useless they looked— like rubble and dust!

"What happened to those pots?" Ayzize asked. "Whose are they?"

"They belong to Sacmis," said Naeem. "He's my rival! Fortunately for me, he hasn't much expertise."

Ayzize stretched his cramped fingers and wriggled his stiff shoulders.

"It's the same with anything," said Naeem. "You must work hard or you can't expect that what you build will be strong enough to survive."

Naeem paused for a long moment. "How is your family?" he asked at last.

Ayzize shrugged. "We're all right." He didn't tell Naeem that both he and his mother ate like sparrows so that the younger children had enough food.

Ayzize sighed silently as he gazed at the pots. How long would it be before his body broke as the pots had broken in the fire? And what would become of his family if he could no longer support them?

Naeem touched Ayzize lightly on the shoulder. "You're a good worker," he said. "I have no fears for my pots."

Naeem's kind words reminded Ayzize of his father. If Ammon could see him now, thought Ayzize, he would be full of pride.

That afternoon, Ayzize felt his father's presence keenly. Perhaps that was why the long coils of clay rolled more easily under his hands. Perhaps that was why he now felt that the clay was not his enemy.

At the end of the day, Naeem looked up from his work. "Come and watch me," he called to Ayzize.

Naeem was decorating a pot, deftly cutting the surface of the vessel with a sharp stick. Ayzize admired the beautiful symmetry of the designs.

"These are all fine pots," said Naeem, waving a hand at the drying vessels. "But without decoration, one is much the same as another."

He turned his attention to the tool in his hand. "It will take many hours to complete the decoration on this pot," he said. "But when it comes time to sell it, it will be worth twice as much as the others." He looked up at Ayzize. "Now off you go. You've earned a good night's rest."

STOP AND CHECK

What important things does Naeem teach Ayzize about working with clay?

Chapter 3
STRENGTHENED BY THE FLAME

Months passed, and a vast stack of pots built up in Naeem's compound. Ayzize turned each one carefully so that it dried evenly in the sun. Naeem continued to decorate the best of them. He showed Ayzize how to rub the sides of others with a smooth stone. Ayzize worked on them until the clay shone like metal. Although Ayzize did not notice it at the time, his back no longer ached, the deep cracks in the skin of his hands had healed, and there was a new strength in his arms. The hours passed more swiftly, running one into another as the sweat poured from his brow.

Sometimes Naeem's wife appeared in the compound with fresh bread, and lately Naeem had taken to sharing it with Ayzize. Very rarely now did the potter's apprentice walk home hungry.

"The pots are ready for firing," announced Naeem one morning. He handed Ayzize a large knife. "I must have wood for the kiln."

For the next two weeks, Ayzize journeyed deep into the thickets around the village to hack down scrub and small trees and drag them back to Naeem's compound. If Naeem noticed his apprentice's weariness, he made no comment. Only Ayzize's mother realized how tired he was and she clucked her tongue when she saw the state of his scratched and grimy body. She fed him like a baby when he arrived at the shelter too tired to hold a spoon.

One morning, on his way to work, Ayzize looked behind him. Over time, the camel trains had made a trail across the land. How he longed to take that well-worn path, to take a different route where work might not be this hard.

Ayzize was still thinking about the possibility of escape when he noticed a strong scent in the air. A plume of smoke was rising above Naeem's compound. The fire!

Naeem would need all the help he could get to maintain its heat. Suddenly, for all his weariness, Ayzize found himself running like the wind toward the village. As he neared the compound, his heart was racing— but not with the effort of the sprint. At last the pots were being brought to life. The fire was the last stage in their long journey, and more than anything, Ayzize wanted to be part of it!

Without being asked, he joined Naeem in his work, and together, they carefully placed more fuel on the sparking fire. By evening, the scrub that Ayzize had spent two weeks gathering had all but disappeared.

"Go home," Naeem told him as the sun began to set. "Tomorrow we shall see what our months of labor have produced."

That night, Ayzize could not sleep. In his mind he saw the shattered pots that Naeem had taken him to see months before. What if all his work—if all his and Naeem's work—were in vain? At last, Ayzize stopped tossing and turning and sat up. Could it be that he now cared as much as his master about the finished pots lying in the ashes?

It was still dark when Ayzize stepped over his sleeping brothers and sisters and padded out of the shelter. By the time he reached the village, the sun was peeking over the horizon.

Naeem was standing beside the spent fire with a piece of brushwood in his hand, and Ayzize watched as he flicked black twigs and charcoal from the silver forms that stood shoulder-to-shoulder like soldiers in the ashes.

"The pots! They're so beautiful," Ayzize breathed.

"And so strong," Naeem replied. "Not one broken."

"I never thought that … that clay could be changed into something so *strong.*"

"And I'll bet you never thought that you, a mere boy, could become a man in just a year," said Naeem.

Ayzize looked down at his feet. He was embarrassed by Naeem's words.

"Did you believe it was possible?" Ayzize asked.

"Your year as my apprentice has taught you much," said Naeem. "I believe you have it in you to be a skillful potter." He paused, as if thinking deeply. "As you know, I have no sons of my own."

Ayzize held his breath.

"Each of us has the power to become the best that we can be," said Naeem. "All we need is a strong base and the strength never to give in. Each of us can come through the fire as a stronger vessel. But you, Ayzize, are like the decorated pot. You are finely crafted. You have more value than the others.

"Will you join me as my partner in this humble business?" asked Naeem. He held out a hand toward the pots that now shone in the first rays of the morning sun. "Will you look on the raw clay as something worthy of your labor?"

Ayzize felt too proud to speak. He *would* join Naeem. Together they would make fine pots, and like his father before him, Ayzize would earn for his family the respect of his village.

"Though heat raged all about you, you survived the fire," said Naeem.

And Ayzize knew that it was true.

STOP AND CHECK

How does Ayzize's thinking and situation change in this chapter?

Respond to Reading

Summarize

Use details from *Wrought by Fire* to summarize what you have learned about how craftsmen helped culture develop. Your graphic organizer may help.

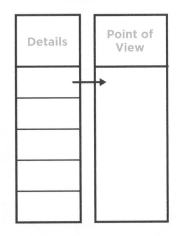

Details	Point of View

Text Evidence

1. What tells you that *Wrought by Fire* is historical fiction? **GENRE**

2. From what point of view is the story told? How does this help you to understand what each of the characters is feeling? **POINT OF VIEW**

3. The suffix *–ful* means "full of" or "having." How does the suffix help you figure out the meaning of the word *skillful* on page 14? **GREEK AND LATIN SUFFIXES**

4. Write from Naeem's point of view in the story. What might he think about having an angry young boy as a helper? **WRITE ABOUT READING**

Compare Texts

Read about how a long-ago craftsman's efforts could influence the development of his culture.

That's Music!

Characters:

ENRICO *(a violin maker)*

SAVINA *(ENRICO's daughter)*

GILBERTO DE LUCA *(a famous violinist)*

> Scene: **ENRICO'S** *violin workshop.* **ENRICO** *is sawing noisily.*

SAVINA: *(shouting from an adjacent room)* Father! What's that terrible noise? I'm trying to study!

ENRICO: What noise? I'm making music!

SAVINA: *(entering)* That's not music! Please stop. *(She exits.)*

> **ENRICO** *sands a violin noisily.*

SAVINA: *(shouting from the adjacent room)* Father!

ENRICO: But I told you, I'm making music!

SAVINA: *(entering)* That scratching isn't music!

17

ENRICO: If I don't finish this violin, we will never be rich and our town will never become famous.

SAVINA: We'll never be rich, anyway.

ENRICO: (*holding up the violin*) But this is no ordinary violin.

SAVINA: It looks like an ordinary violin to me.

ENRICO: This one is different. It is made from the most resonant wood in Italy, the highest-quality glue, and the finest varnish.

SAVINA: But you've been working on it all year. How can you ever be rich if you produce only one violin a year?

ENRICO: Have faith, Savina. Maestro Gilberto de Luca is in town. I believe he is looking for a new violin.

The shop bell jangles, and **GILBERTO** *enters.*

ENRICO: (*bowing*) Maestro! I am honored to meet you.

GILBERTO *bows to* **SAVINA** *and* **ENRICO**. **SAVINA** *curtsies.*

GILBERTO: I'm told that you have a violin I can look at.

ENRICO: I do, Maestro. Would you care to try it out?

GILBERTO: Certainly.

He takes the violin and plays it. **ENRICO** *gasps.* **SAVINA** *claps her hands in delight.*

GILBERTO: This violin … it's … it's unbelievable!

ENRICO: Thank you, Maestro, thank you. Let it be my gift to you, Maestro.

GILBERTO: I couldn't. You're too generous.

ENRICO: I insist. It will be ready for you tomorrow at noon.

GILBERTO: (*leaving*) Tomorrow, then. Good-bye.

SAVINA: Father, how will we be rich if you give away your violins?

ENRICO: Don't worry. When the world hears Gilberto play my violin, every maestro will want one. We will be rich.

SAVINA: Father, now I see. You know how to make money as well as music!

Make Connections

Why are the violins Enrico creates important for his culture? ESSENTIAL QUESTION

When goods are made well, they last longer and attract more buyers. How does the work of Naeem in *Wrought by Fire* and Enrico in *That's Music!* compare? TEXT TO TEXT

Focus on Literary Elements

Flashbacks Flashbacks can be used in both fiction and nonfiction. They are parts of a text that tell what happened in an earlier time than the main story or article.

Flashbacks can provide background to a character or event, or a point of view about events. They can be written in italics to let the reader know the section of text has a different time setting.

Read and Find In Chapter 1 of *Wrought by Fire*, Ayzize pauses and thinks back to the time before his father died, when the family was living well. This is a flashback. It gives readers the background information to understand why Ayzize lives the way he does now, and why it's so important for him to earn money.

The third paragraph on page 7 tells readers that Ayzize had been daydreaming. Ayzize's daydream was a flashback that took him (and the reader) back in time. Now, Ayzize's thoughts return to the work he has to do.

Your Turn

Imagine that Ayzize grew up to be an old man with a successful pottery business. Write a flashback to show what he might think about his time as a young boy, when he was learning his trade from Naeem.